The American Cowboy

THE PITCHFORK RANCH, WYOMING

ENID MORSE, DOUBLE-O RANCH, ARIZONA

AT LAST RANCH, COLORADO

THE COWBOY BAR, MEETEETSE, WYOMING

MICHAEL RUTHERFORD

TEXT BY LARRY FRASCELLA
FOREWORD BY CHARLIE DANIELS

GALLERY BOOKS
An Imprint of W. H. Smith Publishers Inc.
112 Madison Avenue
New York City 10016

The American

Cowboy

ISBN 0 8317 1824 2

CONTENTS

Foreword

Enough words have been written about the American cowboy to fill a considerable dry wash, and enough pictures have been snapped of him to paper the south rim of the Grand Canyon.

Generations of writers, photographers, and artists have churned out megatons of books, movies, television series, paintings, sculptures, and magazine articles extolling the romance of the mysterious figure in the big hat.

Now tell me just what is so romantic about a man who gets up before the sun does seven days a week, mounts some half-rank *caballo* and rides over half of creation chasing stubborn, ornery cattle who'd really rather not be bothered, through cactus and catclaw, rocks and ravines and dust, dust, and more dust.

He lives for weeks on end sleeping on the ground a million miles from nowhere with no television, no shower, and no women.

His world is sweat and saddlesores, horseflies and hangovers, rope burns and rattlesnakes.

All that, and he's paid slightly less than a part-time lightning bug trainer.

So what's it all about then—the national fixation with this ragtag wistful son of the West.

To be honest about it, I just don't know and I seriously doubt if anyone this side of the Pearly Gates does.

But be that as it may, the romance is there, and though I can't tell you why, there are a few things I can tell you about the cowboy.

For one thing he is not to be confused with the razor-cut, bangle-bedecked, two-gun superman who gallops across the silver screen in a silver-mounted saddle, facing down bad men and squiring golden-haired girls with white teeth.

Now I'm not saying that there were no heroes in the Old West. There were plenty of them, and some of them made their living punching cows, but they dang shore didn't glow in the dark.

And for the most part the rodeo cowboy is a different breed, too. Part daredevil, part athlete, he's also a colorful character, but that's another story.

No sir, we're talking about your everyday, garden variety, snuff dipping hombre, commonly known in the horseback world as the working cowboy.

For another thing, he's a man of contradiction. He dances to a different fiddler, looks at the world through a different eye.

What appears to most to be a worthless desolate piece of real estate, to him comes across as "purdy country."

He'll vent his profane vocabulary on any man or animal who gets his dander up, but utter nary an off-color word in the presence of a lady.

He may stay with one outfit for years, then one day suddenly roll his bed, draw his wages, and be on his way, just because he got to wondering what lies over the next ridge.

Money doesn't mean very much to him. Maybe a new pair of packers or a night on the town. Heck, the outfit furnishes three squares a day and all the sky you can sleep under. What else could a feller possibly need?

He doesn't get off his horse unless he has to, and the only time he'll take his hat off is on the dance floor and sometimes when he goes to bed.

He can navigate thousands of acres of mountains and plains with the instincts of a homing pigeon, but would probably be lost his first five minutes in New York City.

Now if you're wondering how I came to these conclusions, I'll tell you.

I've sat in lonely cow camps under a flawless night sky and shared their coffee and conversation.

I've pulled my boots on in the predawn chill and walked to the fire rubbing the sleep from my eyes while the sun was just a rosy suggestion on the eastern horizon.

I've heard the old cook holler, calling the crew to breakfast and the zip of nylon through hondo as the boys tightened their houlihans around their horses' necks.

I've saddled up and trotted out proud, proud of the company I was keeping.

I've viewed God's creations in awe as a fresh day arrived to the music of jingling spurs and the creak of saddle leather.

I've rode the circle and breathed the dust of the branding pens, glad to be just one of the bunch, getting the work done.

I've lain in my bedroll, bone tired, converting sights I'd seen and bits of conversation into memories to cherish for the rest of my life.

I've laughed at their jokes, sought their advice, valued their friendship, and developed a deep and abiding respect for the men who have the guts to live this life of freedom, where there are no unions and no retirement plans.

I've reached out and touched the passion and the dream in the barren expanses of the great American outback, where the moon shines brighter and the mesquite grows.

I've seen it, smelled it, tasted it, and loved it—and yet I can't call myself a cowboy.

That's one honor I'll never be able to claim. But if I could, I'd be proud, I sure would be proud.

Charlie Daniels

BOB EDGAR, OLD TRAIL TOWN, WYOMING

Introduction

They rode out of Texas, according to history, north to Montana and across the Rio Grande. They blazed a trail that marked the boundaries of the Wild West, and at the turn of the century there were thousands of them throughout North America. But by the time photographer Michael Rutherford began his search for the classic cowboy in 1985, there were only a handful to be found, a group of maybe a hundred men by Rutherford's count, scattered across seven states, who might legitimately be called the sons of the original breed.

At first, Mike wasn't sure if any traces of the frontier survived. He had no idea that his impending adventures would be so true to Western form — often thrilling, sometimes harrowing, occasionally comic. He began with a head full of boyhood dreams, the noble stuff he'd acquired from the paintings of Frederic Remington and Charles M. Russell, and old television shows like *The Rifleman* and *Wyatt Earp*. His imagination was fueled by Hollywood, the films of John Ford, the image of John Wayne, and by more recent movies such as *The Long Riders* and *Jeremiah Johnson*. As Rutherford rode the West in his four-wheel drive, he drew inspiration from cassette tapes filled with elegiac Western ballads by Willie Nelson and Waylon Jennings. Over and over, he played tunes with titles such as "Mama, Don't Let Your Babies Grow Up to Be Cowboys" and an ode that increasingly became the soundtrack to Mike's story: "The Last Cowboy Song" by Ed Bruce and Ron Peterson. The chorus contains the words: "This is the last cowboy song/The end of a hundred year waltz/The voices sound sad as they sing by the fire/Another piece of America lost." Yet, eventually Mike would discover that the

WAGON TRAIN

The impression that most people today have of the
Old West comes from TV shows such as *Wagon
Train*, which starred Ward Bond (left) and
Robert Horton.

cowboy was far from extinct. In fact, there was plenty of rip-roaring, rough-riding
life in the old boy yet.

A satisfying definition of a true cowboy is hard to find, especially since
cowboys are given to broad exaggeration and creative mythmaking. H. H. Halsell,
himself a true original, attempted to paint a definitive picture of the cowboy. In his
1937 recollections, he wrote: "the hardships of life qualified him to think for
himself and know how to measure men by correct standards. He was laconic in
speech, using few words to express himself, but his meanings were forceful and
easily understood by his comrades. . . . [He] was clean and had pride because he
knew this life he was leading was all he had, and he made the most of it." As with
most definitions of the cowboy, Halsell's words are warm and heroic, loving *but*
indefinite. The best way to understand the cowboy is to briefly outline his past
and figure out where he came from and why he developed in the first place.

Cowboying can be traced back to an event as pivotal and dramatic as the
Alamo, for it proved to be the turning point in Texas's war for independence. From
that time in 1836, Americans moved onto ranches once owned by Mexicans and
the cattle industry began to spread throughout North America. To drive and tend
the cattle, the men who would become cowboys took over the ways of the
vaqueros, those men who were ranch hands for the Mexicans. (Ironically, when
you consider the legendary "cowboy and Indian" battles that would ensue, many
of those *vaqueros* were mestizos—Indians of mixed blood.) Climbing into chaps
(pronounced "shaps"; from the Spanish *chaparejos*, or—as the Mexicans call
them—*chaparreras*) and picking up a lariat (from the Spanish *la reata*), the
American cowboy was born.

ROUNDUP

Charles Belden

After Texas's War of Independence, the cattle
industry began to spread throughout
North America.

COWBOYS COMING TO TOWN FOR CHRISTMAS

Frederic Remington

At the end of a long cattle drive, cowboys would
typically hit the railhead eager to have fun and
spend their wages.

It took the cattle industry some thirty years to fan out from Texas, using
Texans themselves and men recruited from the East. The year 1866 saw one of
the largest and most famous cattle drives, the drive immortalized by Howard
Hawks, John Wayne, and Montgomery Clift in the 1948 Western film, *Red River*.
During this drive, more than 260,000 longhorns were taken across the Red River
Valley, north and east to Kansas, along the Chisholm Trail. Cattle drives of this
proportion would plant the cowboy firmly in American consciousness.

Changes came quickly for the cowboy, as they did for all Americans. Cattle
towns grew up all over the West, infamous places like Dodge City and Abilene.
Now the cowboy had a public stage for his celebrated antics, the shoot-'em-up,
hard-drinking times for which the cowboy gained renown. These towns gave
birth to legendary figures like Bat Masterson, Wyatt Earp, James Butler ("Wild
Bill") Hickok, and many others. Cowboys always had a great propensity for weav-
ing tales, and separating truth from fiction is hard, even to this day. It was here,
during this heyday of the cowboy, that the stories were born, the type of stories
that would take Michael Rutherford on the road, searching for some taste of the
real thing.

Rutherford himself is a small, stocky man with a neatly trimmed, reddish-
brown beard. There's something impish about him but also something fiercely
determined, fueled by his never-say-die spirit and accentuated by his wild, high-
pitched laugh. When he started his project, Mike wasn't sure how to meet a
cowboy, but his first good contacts came easier than he thought. While working

as a photographer for that gentleman-cowboy, Ronald Reagan, Rutherford met a man who invited him to his ranch in the Montana/Wyoming area. Rutherford took him up on his invitation, and in February 1985 he made his first contact with working cowboys. They told him that if he could uncover one truly traditional cowboy in any state, that man was bound to know the others in his region. For the next three years, Mike periodically set out from his home in Nashville, Tennessee, to see just how many classic cowboys he could find. To that end he traveled to Wyoming, Montana, New Mexico, Texas, Arizona, California, and the high country of northern Colorado. Early in these travels, Mike met a man who told him he'd argue with anyone who said that cowboys were a vanishing breed. "There are lots of cowboys left," the man said, "but there aren't many cow*men* left, men that know cattle, men that know cows. Those men are almost gone."

"Those are the guys I concentrated on," Mike says, "the ones that really knew the old ways. We didn't go for any of those newfangled approaches, no turntables for branding the cattle, no helicopters, no nothing. That's not cowboyin'. A real cowboy wouldn't work on a mechanized ranch. As soon as they'd see a turntable, they'd run."

JAMES BUTLER ("WILD BILL") HICKOK
WYATT EARP

Cow towns like Dodge City and Abeline gave rise
to some of the West's most legendary figures.
including Marshals Wild Bill Hickok and
Wyatt Earp.

GREENHORN

Photographer Unknown

Tenderfeet, like photographer Mike Rutherford, and
the 19th-century greenhorn pictured here, learned
that a cowboy's respect doesn't come easily. It must
be earned.

Mike's indignation about modern ranching comes directly from the cowboys themselves. The original cowboys were men of nature, not men of machines and big business. A cowboy had a close relationship with both cattle and horses, an intimate interaction with the land, and a great taste for solitude. The many changes in the cattle industry since World War I virtually preempted a traditional cowboy's concerns. In the years between the wars, and especially during the depressed 1930s, American ranchers lost their European markets, heavy unemployment caused a general decline in business at home, and natural catastrophes such as hoof-and-mouth disease made their first serious inroads. By the time things improved during World War II, these traumatic events had caused a move toward the relative safety of larger operations and mechanization. Many men adapted to the new ways, but the tried-and-true cowboy had much to lose. As Michael Rutherford searched the country for the original breed, he began to feel that—with all the profound changes progress had wrought—it was less sad that so few cowboys existed and more miraculous that so many of them survived.

As Mike journeyed through cowboy country, he was inspired by the time-lessness of the frontier. He was enlivened by sights as majestic as wild mustangs in the hills, or herds of antelope on the prairie. And he took pleasure in simpler things like finding a town where the blacksmith was still called a farrier, and that farrier was also the sheriff.

Mike began as a tenderfoot; he had much to learn about coping with life on the great frontier. Even something as basic as his size could provide an obstacle, especially when mounting Morgan horses with backsides as high as his head. ("I'd get on them eventually," Mike said, "but then—I'd tell myself—I'm never getting off.") On his first trips, Mike bravely waded through fields of cow manure, thinking that a real cowboy didn't mind. He got stuck in the mud in the middle of No-Man's-Land, before he knew that No-Man's-Land existed. He was attacked by dogs more than once, until he learned to look before leaping from his truck. Through it all, he discovered how to handle a frontier that was rougher than he'd first imagined. He learned how to "cowboy up" his looks and, most importantly, learned how to win the trust of his heroes.

Mike followed the advice of wise old owls like cowboy Bill Tunks, who warned, "Don't go asking a bunch of questions. Don't go prying into family affairs. Let them do the talking. If they want you to know, they'll tell you." The more familiar Mike became with Western ways, the more cowboys he was able to

BOJO'S MEDICINE SHOW

Photographer Unknown

Tom and Peggy Fergusin's "traveling store" in New Mexico has its origins in the 19th century when peddlers roamed the frontier. Some sold badly needed tools and household items while others, like the pitchman pictured here, sold less valuable commodities.

engage, the more fellowship he was able to foster. Before long, he found out that—in most cases—a cowboy makes rapid-fire judgments about strangers. "If a cowboy likes you," Mike says, "he'll invite you in for a talk and a glass of tea before he's even sure of what you are there for."

Along the way, Mike discovered that the West was filled with men like him—those who had a strong affinity for times past. Not all of these citizens could claim to be cowboys; nevertheless they had their own special relationship with the wilder West. Two of those folks were Tom Fergusin and his wife, Peggy (who goes by the nickname "Frog"). They run a traveling store in Clayton, New Mexico. In the old tradition, they go from ranch to ranch, delivering anything that the cowboy wants: pots, pans, saddles, or cat food. Tom is seldom home more than two days a week; the rest of the time he journeys far and wide to provide a service few do nowadays. A mobile general store may not be cost-efficient, but Tom and Peggy are people with a long view. They are committed to the old ways and to a history of which they are proud; and they have found a way to preserve a piece of it in their own lives. Their perseverance spoke volumes about the cowboy and the things for which he stands: simplicity, self-reliance, the spirit of adventure, and personal freedom. Soon enough, Mike realized that accommodation to the past came in as many forms as there are people. Whether it was a foxy old timer like Bill Tunks, a cowboy-turned-entrepreneur like Dave Ericson, a modern dreamer like R.W. Hampton, or a sharpshooting historian like Bob Edgar, these were the people Mike had to meet, the people he had to know.

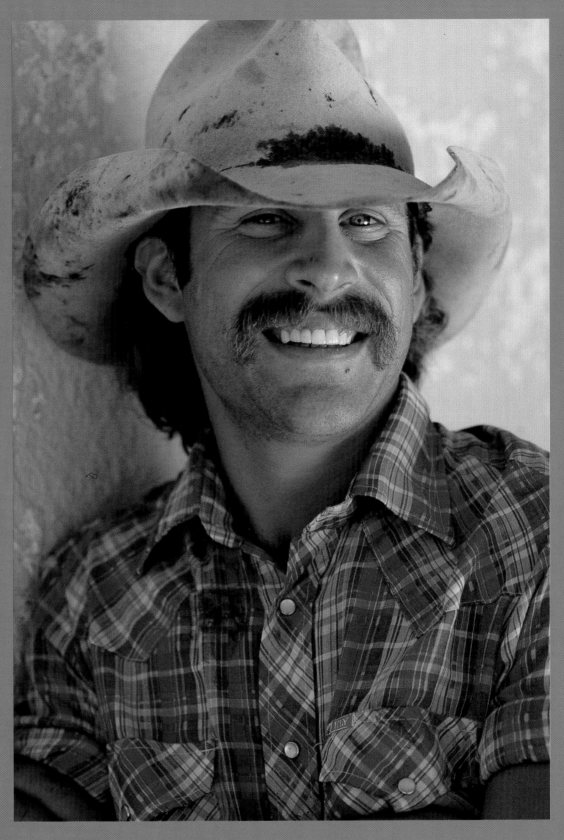

WES LIVINGSTON, TWO-DOT RANCH, MONTANA / WYOMING

MICHAEL RUTHERFORD (CENTER) WITH MIKE LANDUS (LEFT)
AND ENID MORRIS, DOUBLE-O RANCH, ARIZONA

C owboys don't necessarily trust or like people. They think that you're trying to take them. So, if you ever win the love of a cowboy, don't take it lightly.

MICHAEL RUTHERFORD

JOHN UNDERWOOD AND SHIRLEY GOODLOE. CAPITAN. NEW MEXICO

27

CATTLE DRIVE, WYOMING

R. W. HAMPTON, HEINMAN RANCH, TEXAS

DAVE HARRELL, C. S. RANCH, NEW MEXICO

There was not a tree in sight. There was
no vegetation but the endless sage-brush
and greasewood. All nature was gray with
it. We were plowing through great deeps
of alkali dust that rose in thick clouds
and floated across the plain like smoke
from a burning house.

MARK TWAIN
Roughing It

THE FOUR WAY CATTLE COMPANY, TEXAS

BILL TUNKS, THE PALITE I RANCH, WYOMING

THOMAS BROWN, BROWN SHORT HORN COMPANY, NEW MEXICO

GEORGE PROVANCHA, MEETEETSE, WYOMING

The real veteran cowboy was clean and had pride because he knew this life he was leading was all he had, and he made the most of it.

H. H. HALSELL
Texas rancher and Indian fighter
Cowboys and Cattleland

It does make you feel on top of the world for a little while to be shod in a new pair of boots that fit you right. It's surprising what those little things can do for you.

MIKE LANDIS
Double-O Ranch, Arizona

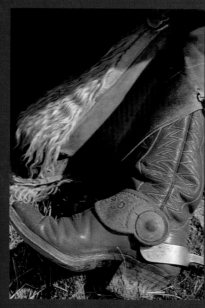

ARCHIE WEST, SANTE FE, NEW MEXICO

Among the thirteen of us we dug up an old fiddle, guitar, and a French harp, enough instruments for plenty of music and singing.

JOHN LEAKEY
19th-century cowboy-cook
The West That Was

THE FLYING W DIAMOND RANCH, NEW MEXICO

MIKE LANDUS, DOUBLE-O RANCH, ARIZONA

I started ridin' saddle broncs. I still think that's the only rodeo event there is. Because that's where it started. A cowboy breakin' a horse.

FRANK SCHWEIGHART
LU Ranch, Wyoming

WES SMITH AND OTHERS, THE FLYING W DIAMOND RANCH, NEW MEXICO

WES SMITH, THE FLYING W DIAMOND RANCH, NEW MEXICO

KIM STUART, THE FOUR WAY CATTLE COMPANY, TEXAS

I guess there's lots of outside work that a man could get into but bein' out on the earth had a lot to do with attractin' me to this kinda work. Maybe its just relating to things on a *real* basis.

JOHN UNDERWOOD
Flying W Diamond Ranch, New Mexico

MIKE MELSON, BLACKSMITH AND FARRIER,
MEETEETSE, WYOMING

GARY LOVELAND, T. O. RANCH, NEW MEXICO

D. B. TRENT, JUNE BUG RANCH, MONTANA

DOUG JOHNSON, T. O. RANCH, NEW MEXICO

The
Storytellers

Bill Tunks is a survivor, if there ever was one. Pushing through his seventies, he continues to work as a cowboy in Meeteetse, Wyoming, a small town in the Big Horn Basin, site of Custer's Last Stand. The area is a veritable gold mine of cowboy lore and legend, as well as the home of a small cluster of real cowboys and historians. As Bill Tunks said, "The Big Horn Basin is where you'll find the last of the best." A natural storyteller, Bill Tunks reminisced about his past in the region and the ways of a cowboy, ways that were tough and wild. He is living proof that an American frontier survives and—to a large degree—remains a place where a man makes his own rules and handles his own situations. "I've never seen any time a fight was settled by the law," Bill said, talking about his years in the Basin. "There were sixteen boys in the Pitt family, as I remember, and I fought every one of them at some time in my life. Sometimes I fought two or three of them at once. We had the law put us in jail, but as soon as we was out, we still had a score to settle. We'd never give up till it was over between *us*." Bill Tunk's voice belies his long history of rough-and-tumble adventures. He speaks in a high, fragile, slightly quavering manner that indicates his years. "The law was fine for what it was meant for," he continued, "but the law isn't meant to come stick their nose into another man's business. If you just leave the men who are fighting alone, they'll go back in the bar, have a drink, and shake hands, no grudge or nothing. In my life, that's how I've seen it turn out."

Bill Tunks lives in a house that was built in the nineteenth century, when the U.S. history of the region began. His house is set far off any main road, and it took Mike and his young assistant, David Bailey, half a day to reach it by truck. "At the

JUDGE ROY BEAN

In the Old West, the law was sometimes a matter of
one's own personal brand of justice. One of the
frontier's more colorful legal interpreters was Judge
Roy Bean, the "law west of the Pecos."

time that house was built," Mike says, "it might take as much as three days to get
there by mule." When they pulled up to the house, Mike noticed a line of buffalo
skulls spread out around the back.

Cigarettes provide one of the last remnants of Bill Tunk's hardiness. He
puffed away, creating clouds of smoke, as he talked and lectured to Mike and
David Bailey. "The sooner the business is settled, the better," Bill said, continuing
his lessons on fair-fighting, cowboy style. "Don't let your anger grow. If you brood
about it, then you're gonna get dangerous. If you can't whip him today, you can't
whip him tomorrow. You might as well give him what you got and get it over with."

Bill Tunks has worked for only a few ranches in his life, although he did his
fair share of short-term horsebreaking throughout the Meeteetse area. He recalls
earlier days when a cowboy didn't earn much for the highly skilled work of breaking a horse. "What could you expect," he said. "Back in the thirties, you could *buy*
a good, broke saddlehorse for as little as fifteen dollars." Bill remembers the
coming of the Appaloosa into his part of the country. "Hell," he said, "I went into
Canada and got them myself." He's seen ranches change hands over and over,
pass down from generation to generation, close down or combine. Sometimes a
large conglomerate simply purchased the land and sat on it—or mined it. In one
rare case, a ranch was bought by the bookkeeper. ("That's what I call working
figures," Bill said. "If I could push a pencil like that, then maybe I could have one
of these outfits.") According to Bill, the Pitchfork was the first ranch in the Big
Horn Basin, founded in 1878 by Otto Franc (or Count Otto Franc von Lichten-
stein). It now belongs to the Hunt family; they own much of the land in the area,
and have since oil baron H. L. Hunt "started buying things up in 1947." These

days, Bill doesn't work as hard as he once did, except in the summer when the Hunt family and their guests are up on a visit.

Besides the famous Hunts, this part of the country served as a home, hideout, and hunting grounds for no less a character than Butch Cassidy. Like many people in the area, Bill Tunks vividly remembers Cassidy and the Hole-in-the-Wall gang. "They made such an outlaw out of him that you expected to see a trail of smoke behind him when he rode over the hill," Bill said, laughing a little at his own description. "But Butch was a grand guy. He never killed anybody in his life. He might rob a bank. Or if he thought somebody had a little too much, he might get them to even it out a little." This wasn't the last time Mike heard someone refer to Butch Cassidy as a Robin Hood of the Wild West.

When it came time to leave, Bill Tunks escorted Mike and David to the front door. As they made their way back to the truck, Bill suddenly yelled out and they whipped around, fearing something was wrong. But Bill waved them on, slightly smiling, and said, "Always remember to stay on the right end of a gun."

The Cowboy Bar in Meeteetse was built in 1891. For decades, it's been the scene of cowboy carousing—"real drinking and loud talk," as one cowboy described it. The ceiling is full of holes, for over the years men have pulled out pistols to prove that they weren't afraid of a bullet's blast, even at close quarters, in tough company, with several beers under their belt. Cowboys come here from all the big

OTTO FRANC RANCH, GREY BULL VALLEY

Joseph Stimson

A view of the Pitchfork Ranch founded by
Otto Franc in 1878.

THE HOLE-IN-THE-WALL GANG

Butch Cassidy (Robert Leroy Parker) is seated on
the right. The Sundance Kid (Harry Longbaugh) is
seated on the left.

ranches in the area. And—as nearly everywhere in the Big Horn Basin—Butch Cassidy was a frequent guest.

When Mike and his assistant, David, entered the Cowboy Bar, they did so with a little trepidation. Bill Tunks had warned them, "You don't want to go in there with a chip on your shoulder because you'll find someboy who'll knock it off." The way Mike tells the story of the Cowboy Bar, it's obvious that he quickly developed the cowboy's flair for hifalutin' horse opera. "I remember going through that swinging door at the Cowboy Bar," he says. "Those boys were yelling and screaming and as soon as we showed ourselves, all the action stopped. They all turned around and stared right at us. We stood there for a minute and then I said 'Hi, boys' and started to explain about being a photographer and all. Well, they just kept staring. We looked all around at their faces, and at the bartender, who had a big scar on his face. We were getting nervous, so I had to think fast. Suddenly, I had an idea. I yelled out, 'Drinks are on me.' Immediately, the talking and yelling started up again. They welcomed us in, and we got some good pictures."

Stories like this one come right out of a Western movie, and they're prevalent throughout the country. From state to state, and town to town, the legends are told and the language is coded. Everyone says they remember who shot whom, but a person's got to dig around and hear a story a few times before he can separate fact from the instant mythmaking that comes natural to these cowboys. In fact, sometimes Mike wondered if facts were the point. Cowboy history is a very personal history, and as Bill Tunks said, "Every story has two sides." Not much is written down, although some ranches kept ledgers which provide a record of the time. But, for the most part, cowboy history runs in a fluid line from the people

THE COWBOYS SALOON
Photographer Unknown
———
Northeastern Wyoming's tribute to the riders of the
range in 1883. with some customers out front.

who've lived it. In some ways, it's not unlike a world much older than the American West, a world where troubadours and wandering minstrels spread the news.

To make fact-finding even trickier, cowboys are known to construct their own histories out of whole cloth. While in Meeteetse, Mike Rutherford met a cowboy called Old George. In his flat-out, direct manner, Old George walked up to Mike and told him that the whole town of Meeteetse had gone to hell. "Why do you say that?" Mike asked. "Well," George answered, "they all died." Mike laughed, and then he noticed the bullet hole in the crown of Old George's hat. When Mike asked him about it, George told him the story. He was up in a bar in Meeteetse and a sharpshooter from Cody came in, took one look at George, and shot him in the head. Luckily, as Old George tells it, the bullet went clear through his hat, in one side and out the other. As far as he's concerned, that hat saved his life and he wears it everyday—hole and all. He wouldn't give it up for anything. Mike loves stories like that, and he collected them all over the West. But he didn't have to travel much farther before he found out the truth about Old George's bullet hole. Just a few miles out of Meeteetse, Mike met Bob Edgar, who innocently related the story of an old cowboy who asked Bob—a well-known sharpshooter in the area—for a favor one evening. "We were in the Elk Horn Bar," Bob Edgar remembers, "and Old George was determined to have a hole shot in his hat, so what was I going to do? He stood there and I blew a hole in it."

That was far from the only pertinent fact Mike Rutherford would receive from Bob Edgar. Bob is well known in the Meeteetse area not only as a crack shot but also as one of the Basin's leading historians. He is the owner and operator of Old

TELLING SOME WINDIES

Charles M. Russell

———

Storytelling is an integral part of the cowboy
tradition. as shown in this early watercolor by
Western artist Charles M. Russell.

WALLACE STREET

Photographer Unknown

Old Trail Town, a re-created frontier town in Cody,
Wyoming, evokes the spirit of places like Virginia
City, Montana, shown here.

Trail Town, a painstakingly preserved re-creation of a cattle town from the turn of
the century. Old Trail Town is the perfect place for Mike, exemplifying as it does
the same urge to preserve the past that motivates own adventures in the Wild
West.

Mike came across the town by accident. It loomed on the horizon like some
Western version of Brigadoon, and he was immediately drawn to it. As he walked
down the dusty main street, Mike was approached by a bearded man. "I thought
he was coming to throw me out." But, instead, Mike was warmly greeted by a
learned gentleman who seemed truly pleased to see him. In his soft-spoken
manner, the man introduced himself, and it was Bob Edgar, who was only too
happy to take Mike through town, relating its history and his own.

Bob is a native of Meeteetse, and spent his early years hunting and trapping
for a living. It was during those years that Bob came up with the idea of Old Trail
Town. As he explains it, "I kept seeing these good-looking old places in the back-
woods getting torn down and burnt up. They were getting destroyed and lost." So
he began the task of moving those classic places off their original sites into one
area where they could be properly maintained. "This collection of buildings is
part of the old frontier days," Bob says. "There are over twenty buildings here that
date from 1879 to 1900. Some buildings have taken ten years to get."

Along the streets of the town are various types of buildings that were and—
in many cases—are necessary to the life of the Frontier West. There's an old
school, store, and blacksmith shop. One cabin was built by a Crow Indian scout
named Curly, who rode with Custer at Little Big Horn. "He escaped just before the

battle started," Bob says, "and died in 1923." Another cabin was a hideout for the Hole-in-the-Wall gang. Through Bob, Mike discovered how Butch Cassidy's gang got its name. "A thirty-mile red wall cliff runs along the east slope of the Big Horn Mountains," Bob Edgar explains. "The highest part is about one thousand feet of sheer wall for most of its length, and you can't get around it either by foot or on horseback. Toward the north end of the wall is a notch, and going through that notch was one of the best ways to get in and out of the area. That notch was made good use of as an exit and a hideout for the Hole-in-the-Wall gang."

Bob and Mike sat for a long time, drinking hot cider on the porch of an old saloon. "This saloon is the oldest one left in this part of Wyoming, built in 1888," Bob said. For every event, Bob had the dates and the details, and he delivered them with a low-keyed air of authority. He knew who built each building and when, what's behind more than one tall tale, and where the bodies are buried— literally. "There's a graveyard on the property where Jeremiah Johnson was re-buried in 1974. Robert Redford, who played him in the movie, came as one of the pallbearers. And there's a buffalo hunter buried there," Bob continued, "named Jim White, pretty well known. He had a long, interesting history, killed around twenty thousand buffalo. We also have his rifle and his cabin—the small one he was murdered at in 1880." Listening to Bob Edgar, it wasn't hard for Mike to imagine gun battles on horseback, train robberies, and old-time church dances. Bob helped Mike make many connections that day, providing the background on many of the names and events he'd hear during his time in the Big Horn Basin. And, thanks to Bob, Mike learned how some men make peace with history.

THE ENTRANCE INTO RED CANYON AND HOLE-IN-THE-WALL COUNTRY

Photographer Unknown

———

This desolate country served as the principal hiding place for one of the West's last—and best known—outlaw gangs.

R. W. HAMPTON, HEINMAN RANCH, TEXAS

The solitude is the best part of being a cowboy. I like to put as many miles between me and the rest of humanity as possible.

RED BASSETT
Ojo Feliz Ranch, New Mexico

MIKE VALDEZ, COLORADO

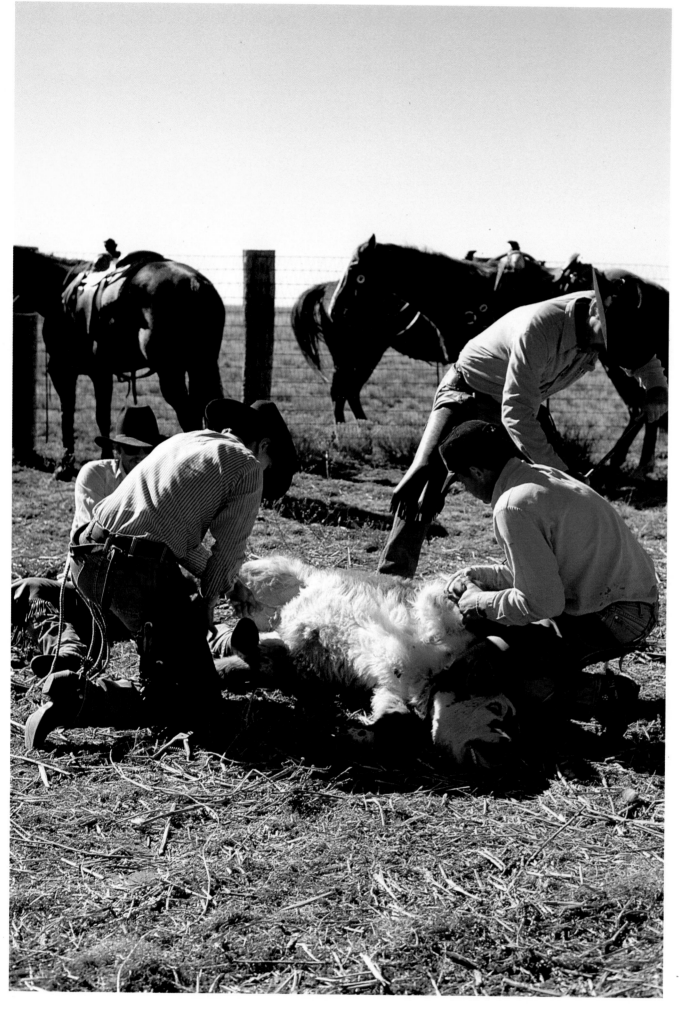

THE DOUBLE-O RANCH, ARIZONA

THE FOUR WAY CATTLE COMPANY, TEXAS

THE FOUR WAY CATTLE COMPANY, TEXAS

ARCHIE WEST, SANTE FE, NEW MEXICO

The bandana was not worn for looks.
It was a useful part of our rigging and we
used it in many different ways. When the
cowhand was away from the ranch house
it was used as a towel. . . . In a pinch it
was used as a tie string or bandage in
case of a wound. It was used to protect
the eyes from the sun glare; by pulling
it close around the neck during a
rainstorm the bandana keeps the rain
from dripping down your neck and
chiling the fins.

HENRY YOUNG
19th-century cowboy

GARY EVERETT, VALLEY VIEW RANCH, COLORADO

JOE ROY RAY, CANADIAN RIVER CATTLE COMPANY, NEW MEXICO

MALOY POOR, LU RANCH, WYOMING

THE COWBOY BAR, MEETEETSE, WYOMING

When we get to drinkin' we do things that maybe we shouldn't do but at the time we think it's okay.

SCOTT McKINLEY
Two-Dot Ranch, Wyoming

75

WES LIVINGSTON, TWO-DOT RANCH, MONTANA/WYOMING

JIM EICKE, BELL RANCH, NEW MEXICO

A GHOST TOWN, ARIZONA

ENID MORRIS, DOUBLE-O RANCH, ARIZONA

79

CARL SCHWERGHART, LU RANCH, WYOMING

A man that don't love a horse, there is something the matter with him.

WILL ROGERS

FRANK SCHWERGHART, LU RANCH, WYOMING

T. O. RANCH, NEW MEXICO / COLORADO

When there's nothing to read
men must talk, so when they were
gathered at ranches or stage stations,
they amused themselves with tales of
their own or other's adventures.

CHARLES M. RUSSELL

ERIC DEWITT AND DAVE ERICSON,
U CIRCLE RANCH, ARIZONA

JIM EICKE, JOE ROY RAY, KEITH LONY, AND TOM FERGUSIN, BELL RANCH, NEW MEXICO

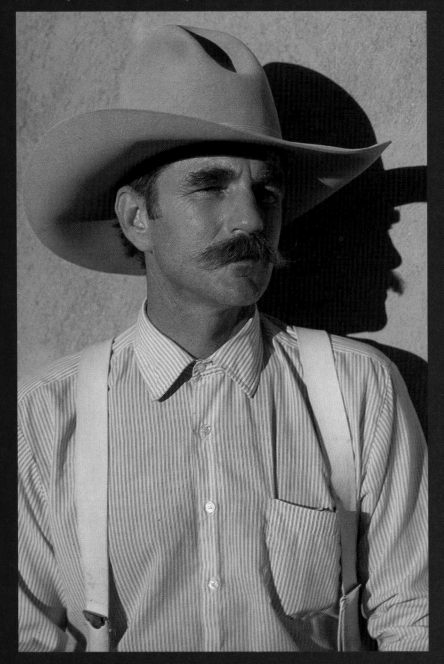

B y the time a cowboy is in his early twenties, he's developed a crease in his hat and a shape to his crown that will never change. He'll have that shape till the day he dies, and a fellow cowboy will know him by that crease, without even seeing his face.

TOM FERGUSIN
ranch supplier
Clayton, New Mexico

DAVE HARRELL, C. S. RANCH, NEW MEXICO

SCOTT McKINLEY, TWO-DOT RANCH, MONTANA / WYOMING

DOC ROBERTS, CROOKED H RANCH, ARIZONA

KEN JAMES, THE BOGLE RANCH, TEXAS

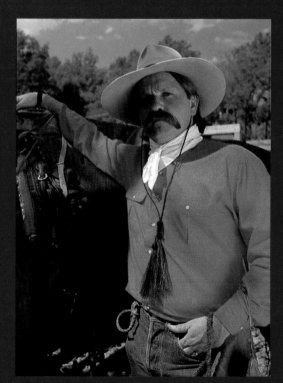

MILES DICKSON, TWO-DOT RANCH, MONTANA / WYOMING

DAVE CORLEW, TWIN PINES RANCH, TENNESSEE

DANNY CALHOUN, HOODOO RANCH, WYOMING

ALDEN B. HART, JR., TWO-DOT RANCH, MONTANA / WYOMING

JOHN FINCH. THE PITCHFORK RANCH. WYOMING

I'll ride the trail till the stars turn pale
And camp at the break of dawn,
Nobody will know which way I go,
They'll only know I'm gone.

BRUCE KISKADOON
"I'm Hittin' the Trail Tonite"
(cowboy poem)

MIKE VALDEZ, COLORADO

JOHN UNDERWOOD, THE FLYING W DIAMOND RANCH, NEW MEXICO

R. W. HAMPTON, THE HEINMAN RANCH, TEXAS

ALDEN B. HART, JR., TWO-DOT RANCH, MONTANA / WYOMING

A chalky taste of dust on the mouth and lips, a gritty sense of earth on the fingers, and an all-pervading heat and smell of cattle...

BRET HARTE
"A Waif of the Plains"

WES SMITH, FLYING W DIAMOND RANCH, NEW MEXICO

Cowboy Style

As Mike soon discovered, the specifics of cowboy life change from state to state, and it's hard to say that anything that holds true for one set of cowboys holds true for another. There are familial relationships, crossovers everywhere, but cowboys resist categorizing. They work hard to distinguish temselves from one another with tactics as large as legend and as small as diamond teeth.

Drawing from his own life experience, Mike says, "Cowboys are a lot like photographers. None of them thinks anyone does it as good as they do." Mike remembers the first time he tripped on this fact, while he was shooting pictures on the Miller Ranch in New Mexico. "This cowboy was carrying his saddle down by his side, so I asked him to pitch it up over his shoulder, and he said, 'Son, that's not the way you carry a saddle.' And I said, 'I saw plenty of boys carryin' a saddle that way in Wyoming and Montana.' 'Yea,' he sneered, 'that's because they don't know how to cowboy up there.' " The range of a cowboy's working methods is being stretched even further these days by new ranching techniques and the presence on many ranches of Australian cowboys who use whips to herd cattle.

Cowboy differences don't end with their working ways. There are also some basic variations in type. For example, no rodeo pictures appear in Mike Rutherford's collection of photographs because, according to Mike, "the professional rodeo cowboy doesn't come off the ranches much any longer. At one time they were all part of the same breed. These days, they've got colleges for professional rodeo riders, and some of your best pro rodeo boys come from the Bronx. The working cowboy can't compete with those hot dog pros. He's out there seven days a week, trying to herd cattle and keep a ranch going." As with any cowboy truth, there are some exceptions; Mike did come across one or two cowboys who

FALLING OFF *A* BUCKING STEER

Photographer Unknown

———

In the Old West, the rodeo served as a test of cowboy
skill. Today rodeo professionals are rarely
ranch hands.

managed to balance working and rodeoing. But, for the most part, rodeo cowboys
are considered a different breed, one Mike decided not to pursue.

Yet, even out on the ranches, there is more than one type of cowboy. In fact,
there is a cowboy who could be as true as the toughest, mangiest son of the
rawhide, even though he jingles more when he walks. They call him a buckaroo,
and he's the ranch's fanciest Dan. The buckaroo may be dressed to the nines with
sterling silver studs on his chaps, a fancy kerchief twisted round his neck, extra-
special work on his boot leather, and jinglebobs that make his spurs ring
louder—but he's a real working cowboy nevertheless. "He's just more into show,"
Mike says.

Yet, the buckaroo is merely the most obvious embodiment of a trait extant
among cowboys: their pride in uniform. Most cowboys are neatly—almost
ritualistically—attired, always donning a hat and dressed in a long-sleeve shirt.
("Wearing a short-sleeve shirt is a disgrace," Mike says.) Aside from the suspend-
ers worn on the Quien Sabe Ranch in Texas, most cowboy gear comes down to a
few classic items such as boots, hats, and chaps. They are the clothes a cowboy
lives and works in, and they are all necessary to getting the job done. For example, chaps—those long leather leggings a cowboy wears—are a popular fashion
on some city streets. But on a ranch they are needed to cut down on saddle sores
and protect the legs from the briers, weeds, and cactuses that thickly populate the
rough country which cowboys tear through while moving cattle. There are almost
as many styles of chaps as there are styles of cowboy. In the North, where the
countryside is not as rough, cowboys tend to wear chinks, which are shorter. In
the South, some cowboys wear shotgun chaps, which are tight to the leg, and

others wear batwings, the type of chaps that fan out on the sides to provide extra protection. A top-notch buckaroo might wear woolies, which are a fancy, fur-covered form of chaps.

Boots are also a major part of a cowboy's paraphernalia and equally important to their work. Cowboys have strong feelings about their boots and take great pride in their sturdiness and workmanship. For a worker who does not earn much, a cowboy will go out on a limb for a good pair of boots. Mike remembers one cowboy who said, "When I need a new pair of boots, I've got to get a loan. And just about when the loan is paid up, I need a new pair." "A good pair lasts them about a year," Mike says. "They need to be tough and usually worn with their pants tucked in." "A cowboy's boots gotta be tight," according to David Harrell, a friend of Mike's who has cowboyed in British Columbia. "They're supposed to be hard to get on. And they've got to be tall; they wear tall boots in the West, made of shark, elephant, or bull hide. That's what's real popular."

Belt buckles are equally important. ("Every buckle tells a story," according to one cowboy.) An assortment of knives are carried: fancy types with handles of rosewood and ivory, or file knives which are made out of the old files a blacksmith uses. ("They hold their edge perfectly," says Mike.) Of course, every cowboy owns his own saddle. He's expected to carry it onto a ranch if he wants to get work. A cowboy and his saddle have a close relationship and, as Mike points out, "It's gotta fit his butt to a tee."

Around his neck, a cowboy usually wears a colored kerchief called a wild rag. A cowboy can use a wild rag for just about anything from earmuffs to tending wounds when he's out for days driving cattle. But, for the most part, wild rags are

MOUNTED COWBOY

John C. H. Graybill

This fellow, photographed by John C. H. Graybill in the 1880s, typifies the vanishing breed that one of today's punchers had in mind when he said, "There are lots of cowboys left, but there aren't many cow*men* left."

WYOMING COWBOY

Charles D. Kirkland

All decked out in his fancy gear is this
impressive cowpoke.

draped around the mouth and nose to protect the rider from dust in the summer
and cold in the winter. Usually a cowboy sticks to the same color once he's
chosen it.

Probably the most beloved and individual aspect of a cowboy's look is the
way he wears a hat. Whether it's a Stetson, straw, or ten-gallon hat, a cowboy
works it into a personal signature. A cowboy might adopt a deep crease down the
middle or create a Montana top, which makes the crown look like the tip of a
Phillips screwdriver. The cowboy is equally sensitive to a hat's durability and
weight, and the width of its brim. As traveling-store owner Tom Fergusin said, "By

the time they're in their early twenties, cowboys have developed a crease in their hat, a crown, and a shape that they'll never change. They'll have that shape till the day they die; and a fellow cowboy will know that man by that crease, without even seeing his face."

As Mike traveled from ranch to ranch, talking to cowboys and gathering information, he noticed that variations in a cowboy's style were followed by distinctions in lifestyle. While many of the truest cowboys remained nomads and loners, Mike discovered a new type of cowboy along the way, a traditional cowboy for the 1980s. This cowboy respects the past and strives to play by its rules, but he has made an adjustment to the modern world. Steady, stable, and respectable, this cowboy usually has a wife and family and a strong relationship with one ranch and the Lord. Although most ranches only have room for a few married cowboys, ranchers are happy to see this new breed come along. As in much big business and corporate practice, a married man sticks around because of his family. In the cowboy's case this responsibility might translate into a job commitment of a year or two.

WHEN TWO COWBOYS MEET ON THE RANGE
Charles Belden

Both of the cowboys pictured here are wearing chaps, but note the elaborate studding on the chaps of the fellow at left. Incidently, these same chaps can be seen in a contemporary setting on page 50.

For the most part, women show up in the cowboy landscape as the wives of these boys (although that's not the only role they play: there are women who run ranches and who work as foremen and cowhands. In Mike Rutherford's assessment, "Women are different in the West. There aren't many of them unless you go to the bigger towns which the cowboys tend to avoid. There *are* women who go hunting down cowboys looking for the last of the real breed men. They want to become cowboy wives, and that isn't an easy life. If a cowboy is getting up to run cattle at 3:30, his wife is up before him, having breakfast ready by the time he needs it."

Mike found his favorite clean-cut, family cowboy in the person or R.W. Hampton. "He's a cowboy from the word go," according to Mike Rutherford, "a vibrant fella, a good Christian, and a man who loves nature and the land." In many ways, R.W. is the very embodiment of the correct cowboy. He came up through the proper ranks, having been trained on the Philmont Ranch, where cowboys are taught the basic skills of their trade. The Philmont Ranch is the closest the West has to a cowboy college. There, a young man learns to rope and heel a steer, ride a bull, take a fall, and cook his own food. According to Mike, "After three or four summers, the majority of boys quit, but there are always ones like R.W. who go on."

Hampton is also the kind of cowboy that's been discovered by Hollywood and Madison Avenue—and that's okay with him. He has no trouble making the transition from the bright lights of Hollywood back to the natural light on the ranch. He's been in several films, including one of Kenny Rogers's "Gambler" movies, and he was the Levi's cowboy for years. "He certainly doesn't mind being photographed," says Mike, who met R.W. on his first trip into cowboy country and has documented his sharp outfits and handlebar moustache for years. R.W. is proud of the way he looks, although Mike says, you'd never mistake him for a buckaroo.

The success of R.W. Hampton proves how far a canny cowboy can go while still adhering to the traditional ways. Hampton works on the Heimann Ranch in the Texas and southern New Mexico area. The Heimann Ranch consists of 110 sections, 640 acres to each section. It's owned by three Heimann brothers and their father, whose forebearers homesteaded the ranch in 1907. Through diligence, R.W. now runs an entire section of the ranch—once owned by the Heimann grandmother. In return, R.W. gets a house for his wife and son. This arrangement allows R.W. the freedom to keep his own time, and come and go as he pleases, as long as the cattle are tended. It is an enviable setup for any cowboy.

R.W. indulges in yet another great tradition of cowboy life, one that stretches in popular culture from Gene Autry to Willie Nelson—that of the singing cowboy. Music is important to a cowboy; folk art and entertainment remains a large part of his life. Although some of the younger guys are given to watching TV, soap operas especially, Mike hardly ever saw a television set in the homes he visited. And when he did, it was never turned on. ("Don't forget," Mike says, "sometimes the types of places I searched out didn't even have electricity or a telephone. They ran things on kerosene lanterns and cooked their food on a wood fire.") Cowboys provide themselves with their own entertainment, especially when they're out on a cattle drive. Herding cattle is a slow business, and it's out of these quieter times that the cowboy song and the poem were born. It's a tradition that still continues strong. "There's some competition," Mike points out, "to see who can come up

COWBOYS

Charles Belden

The cattle drive may have given birth to the cowboy
song, but strumming proved a pleasurable way to
pass the time back at the ranch as well.

with the best song, the funniest poem, or the meanest one." R.W. has written many songs and has high hopes that someday they'll be heard by a larger public. The last time Mike visited R.W., he played a self-penned ballad that summed up the feeling of this new breed of family cowboy, a man in touch with the Lord and more gentle and gentlemanly in his ways. That night, R.W. played:

Gather round boys and I'll sing you a song.
The words they are simple. It shouldn't take long.
You ride the cattle o'er the mountains and plains.
Take time to ponder just who sends the rain.
For the rain in the spring brings the summer to bloom,
with the sun burning warm and the heavenly blue.
Then autumn brings winter, the ice and the snow.
That's His perfect circle and so on it goes.
From the four winds that blow to the whippoorwill call,
From the green leaves of spring to the gold of the fall.
Sunrise and sunset and all in between,
The Master's in everything that you see.

THE FOUR WAY CATTLE COMPANY, TEXAS

BILL BIRD, THE FLYING W DIAMOND RANCH, NEW MEXICO

THE FLYING W DIAMOND RANCH, NEW MEXICO

TERRY OVERMYER, NEW MEXICO CATTLE COMPANY, NEW MEXICO

Some guys punch cows for seven or so years and think they're cowboys. You can't hardly learn to shoe a horse in seven years. It takes a long time to be a real cowpuncher.

DAVE ERICKSON
U Circle Ranch, Arizona

DAVE CORLEW, TWIN PINES RANCH, TENNESSEE

RICK WALT AND HIS SON JEFF. MILLER RANCH. NEW MEXICO

He is proud that he is a horseman, and
has contempt for all human beings who
walk. . . . The cowboy does not walk,
and he is proud of that fact.

PHILIP ASTON ROLLINS
The Cowboy

OJO FELIZ RANCH, NEW MEXICO

DENNIS SCHUTZ AND MIKE VALDEZ, AT LAST RANCH, COLORADO

VALLEY VIEW RANCH, COLORADO

CATTLE DRIVE, WYOMING

My ceiling is the sky, my floor is the
   grass,
My music is the lowing of the the herds
   as they pass;
My books are the brooks, my sermons
   the stones,
My parson is a wolf on his pulpit of
   bones.

"The Cowboy"
(cowboy song)

SCOTT McKINLEY TWO DOT RANCH MONTANA/WYOMING

Lone Star belt buckles and old faded
   Levis
And each night begins a new day
And if you don't understand him
And he don't die young
He'll probably just ride away.

ED BRUCE and PATSY BRUCE
"Mammas Don't Let Your Babies Grow Up to Be Cowboys"
(contemporary song)

CODY PRICE, THE FOUR WAY CATTLE COMPANY, TEXAS

TWO-DOT RANCH, MONTANA / WYOMING

BILL BIRD, FLYING W DIAMOND RANCH,
NEW MEXICO

PREZ VALDEZ, PAGOSA SPRINGS, COLORADO

"PAPPY" YOCHIM. TWIN PINES RANCH. TENNESSEE

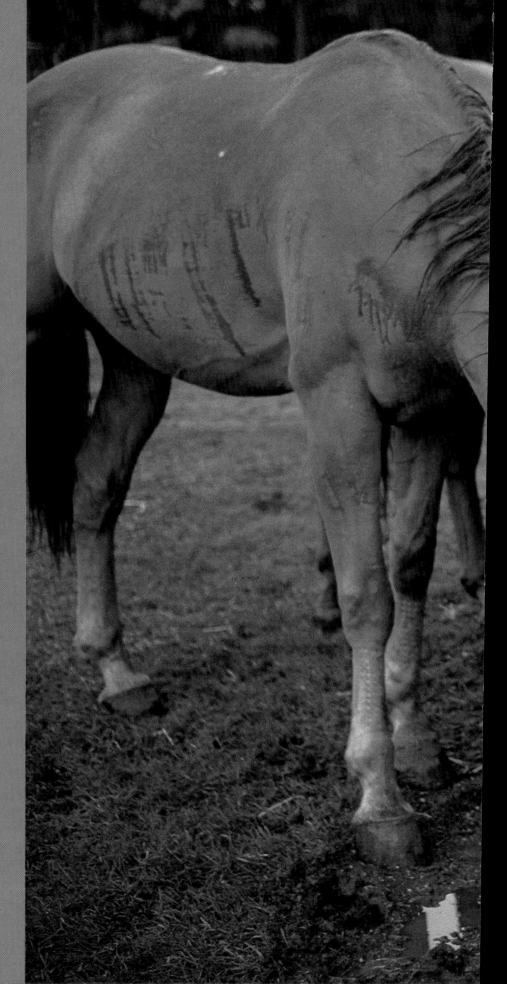

Every horse is an individual and you have to treat him as such. They're like people. They've got their own personalities.

R. W. HAMPTON
Heinman Ranch, Texas

JIM EICKE, JOE ROY RAY, KEITH LONG, AND TOM FERGUSIN

MALOY POOR, LU RANCH, WYOMING

SHIRLEY GOODLOE, CAPITAN, NEW MEXICO

ENID MORRIS, DOUBLE-O RANCH, ARIZONA

DON CATES, THE FOUR WAY CATTLE COMPANY, TEXAS

WES LIVINGSTON, TWO-DOT RANCH, MONTANA / WYOMING

BILL OWENS, A-WEST RANCH, ARIZONA

They do not walk well, partly because they so rarely do any work out of the saddle, partly because their chaparejos or leather overalls hamper them when on the ground.

THEODORE ROOSEVELT
Cattle Country of the Far West

RED BASSETT, OJO FELIZ RANCH, NEW MEXICO

MIKE VALDEZ, AT LAST RANCH, COLORADO

132

JAY YORK, FREE-LANCE BRONCOBUSTER

FUZZY SMITH, MILLER RANCH, NEW MEXICO

133

Punching cattle is the most highly skilled, underpaid occupation on earth. It takes a lifetime of learning. And if you've stopped learning, you've lost the fire.

R.W. HAMPTON
Heinman Ranch, Texas

DONN DAVIES, C. S. RANCH, NEW MEXICO

TEXAS RANGE. SUNRISE

Men
At Work

R. W. Hampton represents a real success story among cowboys. But for many of these men, life was tougher and more precarious. Like farmers throughout the United States, many ranchers are struggling to keep their homesteads alive. As a result, a cowboy with a family might get as little as $400 a month, and a milk cow for his baby. One unidentified cowboy said, "If you're a cowboy, you're supposed to work for less pay just for the privilege of riding a horse. That's how it's always been, and cowboys never organized because it would threaten their freedom of life. Besides, you can't get three cowboys to agree on nothing." At its worst, a bad economic situation pushes many cowboys into new types of work. "But it kills them," Mike says, "to take a regular job."

Yet, the cowboy endures. And if a person were to ask why, one answer sits squarely on the bottom line: there remains an economic need for a man with his expertise. No matter how mechanized a ranch may become, horses still need to be broken and cattle still need to be driven over terrain too tough for any four-wheel drive to survive.

It was this kind of toil that forged Mike Rutherford's last great link with the cowboy. Mike found his truest understanding of the cowboy by going beyond the talk and the picture-taking and by becoming a working cowboy himself. Mike broke into the cowboy's ranks at the L-U Ranch in Wyoming where he was asked to be part of a cattle drive.

"We had to go 25 miles a day for three days," Mike remembers, "moving 1500 head of Black Angus with only five cowboys. We went to the pens before the sun

A REAL LIVE COWBOY

T. W. Ingersoll

———

"If you're a cowboy," says one modern ranch hand,
"you're supposed to work for less pay just for the
privilege of riding a horse. That's the way it's
always been."

came out. It was maybe 18–20 degrees. There was steam rolling off the cattle, and my beard was all frosted up. We got them going and kept them moving most of the day."

This was the beginning of much firsthand cowboy action that Mike would experience; and the more he worked, the more he learned about the underpinnings of a cowboy's job. During his drive at the L-U, Mike learned a great deal about why and how cows are herded. "The law insists you do that to keep the land from getting overgrazed," Mike says, "and you've got to abide by these laws. Down in the South, they also move cattle for water, especially through the summer. They start out low in the spring and work the cattle up into high country. The terrain is rough and rocky, and it's real hard work. It might take you all day to move five cows up the hillside, back into where water might be."

On cattle drives in the Northwest, the goal each day is to reach the line shacks which are set up along the trail. There, a cowboy can rest up and sleep. Line shacks range in size and condition from old trailers to small houses. "Of course, that's the fancy way of trail driving," Mike says. In the more Southern areas, cowboys still sleep outside or in tents. "During our trail drive with the L-U," Mike says, "we had to sleep on the ground with scorpions, fire ants, and diamond-back rattlers galore."

COWBOYS AT CAMP

Charles Belden

On cattle drives in the Northwest, line shacks were
set up along the trail. Typically cabins were
separated from each other by an average day's ride.

THE MESS WAGON
Laton Alton Huffman

The chuck wagon was the hub of the cattle drive, the
main gathering point for cowboys coming in from
the trail.

At dusk, the drivers round up the cattle, and one or two men stay awake with them, standing guard. This was done in the past because of cattle rustlers. "And believe it or not," Mike says, "that still goes on. It's serious business, especially if they're caught." A rustler isn't always the easiest criminal to find because once he captures a cow he puts a different brand on it, something that's a variation of a preexisting mark.

Through all his firsthand experience, Mike remained excited whenever he discovered traces of the past. In some cases, an old chuck wagon might be part of a driving team. Yet there are only a few places—like Babbitt's Ranch in Arizona— that work wagons and have a wagon boss. To his chagrin, Mike learned that a wagon is not used for sleep. It is used to carry supplies, like bedding and pots. Many times in his journeys, Mike had to stay in old bunkhouses where single cowboys still spent their nights, playing cards, and dressed in red flannel long johns. These houses were often infested with skunks and subject to many other manifestations of nature. Mike recalls his stay at the Two-Dot Ranch on the Montana border. "It was the middle of winter and the bunkhouse was up on stilts. The whole house was only the size of a bed, and you had to spread out your own bedroll. During the night they had these wind storms called chinooks. It's a warm wind that can melt a heavy snowfall over night. And the wind comes in at 60–70 miles an hour. And, I swear, it was rocking that bunkhouse. Needless to say, we didn't sleep very well that night."

During his time as a ranch hand, Mike learned one of his most important lessons: that dead center, at the heart of every cowboy, was his love and knowledge of horses and cattle. In his recollections of the Golden Age, cowboy R. D. Symons wrote: "A good man and a good horse are a working team in which loyalty, forbearance, trust, and affection all work together for the good, be that man or horse of any color. . . . To separate a good man from a good horse of his breaking is like parting man and wife." In order to become a cowboy, common wisdom goes, you have to grow to the saddle. "Life goes easier for a man when he's on a horse," said one cowboy who "stuttered up a storm" until he was on horseback. Once off the ground, "he spoke just fine."

Feelings run high about cattle, too—especially when it involves the type of cow that's tended. "Some cowboys wouldn't be caught dead with Charolais cattle," Mike says, referring to an increasingly popular breed of small, light-colored cattle that are thought too dainty for some cowboys' taste. Cattle is also the subject of geographic prejudices. "In the Northwest," Mike says, "they mostly run Hereford and pure Black Angus. In the Southwest, cowboys work with brown cows and Brangus, a mixed breed culled from the mating of a Brahma bull—the old humpbacked Brahma bull—and the Angus. As Mike tells it, "Many cowboys would rather have a mixed breed cow than a thoroughbred because they catch diseases less easily; they're heartier."

This was the type of information Mike figured he'd find on the trail, but occasionally he learned a lesson he didn't expect. It was master cattleman Ed Lemmon who wrote, "I think it must've been born in cowboys to like a good joke." Mike discovered cowboy humor with a stinging vengeance on the first driving day with the boys of the L-U. "When I was preparing for the cattle drive the next day, this cowboy comes over to me and says, 'Mike, you need to go to the store and get

COWBOY GAME

Charles Belden

Whether it's making up stories, kidding a tenderfoot, or playing a game of five-card stud, cowboys welcome lighthearted moments like the one pictured here to provide relief from the rigors of the puncher's life.

yourself some Tough Skin,' which is stuff that you spray on your feet for callouses and such. And this cowboy said, 'When you get up in the morning spray that stuff all over your legs, butt, and thighs and you won't get no saddle sores. That'll make those guys think you're as tough as knotty wood.' So, I thought it was a great idea. I could tell the boys were a little concerned about mine and David's riding talents. So I figured I'd show them. I thought, 'Boy, wait till those guys see me on a horse.' I got up that morning about 3:30, and it was cold. I asked David if he wanted some Tough Skin but he didn't think he needed it. I still thought it was a great idea, so I soaked myself down with it, all over, and I pulled on my long johns and jeans and chaps. But when I went out and got on the horse, I noticed a lot of pain. After an hour or so, I was about to die. I asked David how he was doing and he says he's feeling fine—which didn't make sense because I'd had a lot more riding experience than he had. So I just kept riding along, wondering why I felt so bad. And by the end of the day, I was really hurting. When my legs hit the ground, my knees gave way. Then we realized what the problem was. The Tough Skin was like glue, and all day long my hair was ripping out of my body. I was almost in tears. I don't know how I made it for sixteen hours. They had to peel those long johns off me."

Luckily, not all of Mike's lessons were so painful and embarrassing. And soon enough, he grew accustomed to the rugged, wild ways of many cowboys. Some of the toughest cowboying Mike experienced was at the U-Circle Ranch in Arizona, owned by Dave Ericson. Ericson is known to run a tight ship and to be especially hard on young cowboys. He is one of the most famous, rough, and robust cowboys left in the West, renowned across four states. At one point, Ericson was a championship all-around cowboy, a rodeo rider and rancher. Legend says he's the man who got all of the wild burros and cattle out of the Grand Canyon. Now he has become a prosperous landowner in his own right. Mike remembers his first moments on Ericson's ranch with a mixture of laughter and trepidation. "Once you leave the pavement, it's an hour and a half ride over boulders in my truck, back to Ericson's place in a holler. As I was riding, I suddenly saw this ball of smoke rising over the hills. As it got closer, I saw that it was a truck that had this big old boy in a ten gallon hat sitting in it. I waved and he seemed real leery. 'Can I help you boys?' was the first thing he said. And I said, 'We're here from Nashville, to shoot you.' He looked suspicious and said, 'Do I know you from anywhere in my past?' 'No. But we called and said we was coming and your wife was supposed to tell you about it.' 'Well,' he says, 'I would think that on something like that she would have talked to me but she never mentioned nothing.' He was very kind and calm and said, 'Why don't you come down to the house and we'll talk about this.' So I never thought another thing about it till the next day on the trail when Dave Ericson suddenly lets out this big laugh. He said, 'I have to tell you boys. Nobody told me about any photographers and for awhile I thought you were here to kill me. I'd been hoping that when the time came, you might be fair enough to give me a chance to shoot you back.' " That story continues to raise a little hair on the back of Mike's neck, but it was indicative of the hardiness of life with Dave Ericson. "He's the true cowboy breed," Mike says. "There are maybe twenty men who could stack up to him."

Mike joined Dave Ericson's men as they ran pack mules into the hills. They were delivering supplies to cowboys who'd been moving cows to water for over a month and a half. Mike remembers the undomesticated conditions he found there. "When we arrived at the camp," Mike says, "we were thirsty, and they pointed to the trough that the horses and dogs drank out of, and that's where we drank. After they ate, they'd hand you the plate and fork, and say, 'Here you go, we only have three plates up here.' They'd eat potatoes all the time, and they'd eat some beef if a cow broke its leg or if they came across a tough old bull. Boy, that was tough meat. Tough like jerky."

Mike discovered that besides all the sweat and discomfort, cowboying could also be dangerous work. Mike heard a fair share of stories about men who broke their necks when horses fell over backward, or three-fingered cowboys who lost their digits by flipping a lasso the wrong way while on a roping horse. Throughout his adventures, Mike came to understand the truth behind R. W. Hampton's words: "Punching cattle is the most highly skilled, overworked, and underpaid occupation on earth."

Mike remembers one incident that dramatically underscored the wide-ranging importance of a cowboy's work. It occurred on the T-O Ranch in New Mexico. It was the end of the day, and Mike and David and the rest of the boys were exhausted after a long haul. Everybody was looking forward to the delicious spread one cowboy's wife had laid out. By the time they sat down, dinner was already cold but they didn't mind. Then, as soon as they began to eat, the ranch foreman came running in, all excited and yelling, "Grab your knives, boys, let's go." As Mike tells it, "The cows had gotten into a field of alfalfa and they'd gassed

ZACK T. BURKETT, FOREMAN OF THE LS OUTFIT, OVERLOOKING THE CANADIAN RIVER FROM A HIGH POINT

Erwin E. Smith

———

"There's a big difference between the cowboy who does what he does for a living and the cowboy who does it for nothing," says one modern puncher. "Cowboyin' is just what you do and who you are."

up with a condition called bloat. It's one of the worst things that can happen to a cow. It can kill them. The cowboys had to get out there, and one by one, take each cow, get down, and make a two- to six-inch gash in its side and squeeze the stuff out of 'em. It's the only thing that can save their lives. We were pretty successful, although they did lose a few that night. We were out there till eleven, and we had to get up at four the next morning." When they finally headed back in for the night, the foreman turned to Mike and David and said, "Boys, that's what we mean when we say, 'Cowboying is 24 hours a day, seven days a week.' "

Mike was forever amazed at the depth of a cowboy's knowledge and the breadth of his duties. Yet, despite the never-ending need for his services, the true cowboy's numbers continue to decline. Some men remain certain that the cowboy will see better days. One ranch hand said, "There will come a time when a cowboy is paid what he's worth, just to have him there. I've seen it change in my lifetime.... For a ranch to operate well and efficiently, they're gonna have to cater to the man with the knowledge of getting it done."

Whether that statement represents false hope or proves to be true, it possesses the grit and tenacity that sets the cowboy apart. These were qualities Mike learned to admire as he drew closer to the cowboy, as he came to know him more as a man and less as a myth.

One afternoon, toward the end of his travels, Mike found a particularly gregarious bunch of ranch hands and asked them to name those things that make a cowboy's life worthwhile. "A new hat and a new pair of boots always makes the sun shine a little bit brighter, the day a little shorter," said one. "I like to put as many miles between me and the rest of humanity as possible," said another. That sentiment was immediately echoed by a third cowboy who said, "If I didn't know that I could ride over that hill and not see another soul, I'd go crazy." Then, one cowboy stopped the conversation by saying, "There's a big difference between the cowboy who does what he does for a living, and the cowboy who would do it for nothing. Cowboyin' is just what you do and who you are."

BILL BIRD, FLYING W DIAMOND RANCH, NEW MEXICO

They toss their ropes and catch the bull's feet, they skillfully avoid his rush, and in a spirit of bravado they touch his horns, pat him on the back, or twist his tail.

FREDERIC REMINGTON

M. L. JAMES AND KEITH JAMES, QUIEN SABE RANCH, TEXAS

ENID MORRIS, DOUBLE-O RANCH, ARIZONA

OLD TRAIL TOWN, CODY, WYOMING

CODY PRICE, THE FOUR WAY CATTLE COMPANY, TEXAS

TWO-DOT RANCH, MONTANA / WYOMING

T. O. RANCH, NEW MEXICO

Each man filled his plate with navy beans, sow belly, biscuits and a cup of coffee—no cream or sugar for the cowboy's coffee. Some men live to eat; a cowboy eats to live.

H. H. HALSELL
Texas rancher and Indian fighter
Cowboys and Cattlehands

JOHN UNDERWOOD, THE FLYING W
DIAMOND RANCH, NEW MEXICO

152

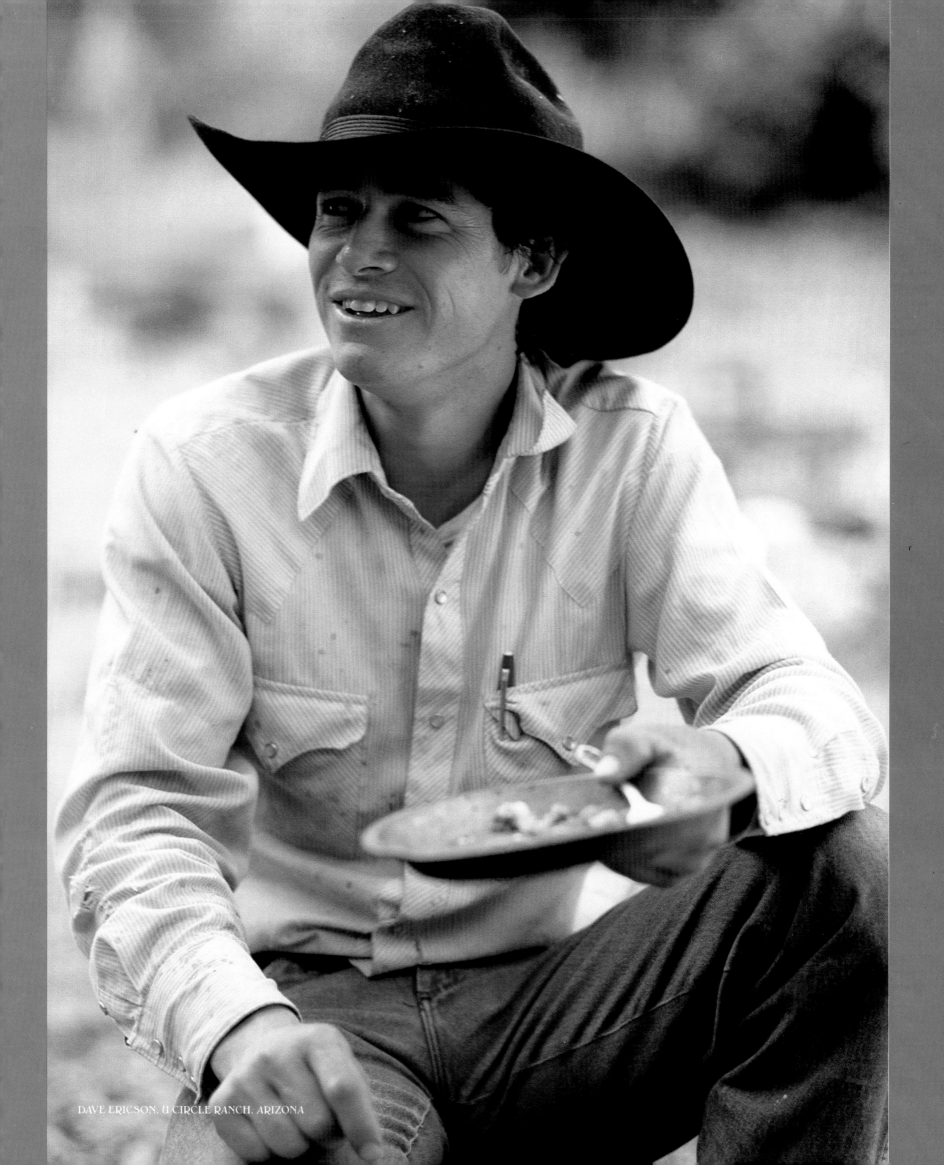

DAVE ERICSON, U CIRCLE RANCH, ARIZONA

TODD ESTES, HOODOO RANCH, WYOMING

I jumped in the saddle and grabbed holt
   the horn
Best blamed cow-puncher ever was born.

I popped my foot in the stirrup and gave
   a little yell,
The tail cattle broke and the leaders
   went to hell.

I don't give a damn if they never do stop:
I'll ride as long as an eight day clock.

The Old Chisholm Trail
(cowboy song)

MALOY POOR. TRAIL DRIVE THROUGH THE BADLANDS, WYOMING

THE VALDEZ RANCH, PAGOSA SPRINGS, COLORADO

TRIPLE T RANCH, NEVADA

THOMAS BROWN,
BROWN SHORT HORN COMPANY,
NEW MEXICO

DOUG JOHNSON, T.O. RANCH, NEW MEXICO

161

ARCHIE WEST, SANTE FE, NEW MEXICO

The terrible grip of the blizzard,
When the horse and the rider reel;
The curse of the snow-blind puncher
And the frostbites that throb and peel,
The nights you hate to remember,
Out in line camp alone,
When the gray wolves howl in the timber,
And the perishing cattle moan.
You tried to keep track of the slaughter,
But the frost and the storm were kind;
How you chopped the ice from the water,
And prayed for an early spring.

BRUCE KISKADOON
"Between the Lines"
(cowboy poem)

SNOW RUN, COLORADO

BOB REEVES, FLOWERPOT RANCH, ARIZONA

BARNEY COPPEDSE, T.O. RANCH, NEW MEXICO

If not breaking horses, mending saddles, or doing something else of the sort, the cowboys will often while away their leisure moments by practicing with the rope.

THEODORE ROOSEVELT
Ranch Life and the Hunting Trail

ALDEN B. HART, JR., TWO-DOT RANCH, MONTANA / WYOMING

DANNY LOVE, DICKIE RANCH, WYOMING

S winging a rope is all right, when your neck ain't in it, then it's hell.

WILL ROGERS

M. L. JAMES, QUIEN SABE RANCH, TEXAS

GOING TO COW CAMP, U CIRCLE RANCH, ARIZONA

A fella said, "There's not many of you left, is there? Cowboys is a dyin' way of life." I told him, "No sir, we just been keepin' the best for ourselves."

JOHN UNDERWOOD
Flying W Diamond Ranch, New Mexico

172

The cowboy is now gone to worlds invisible; the wind has blown away the white ashes of his camp fires; but the empty sardine box lies rusting over the face of the western earth.

OWEN WISTER
The Virginian

I want to thank my wife and sons for their love and understanding, and for enabling me to pursue this dream even though it took me away from them for long periods of time.

And a special thanks to David Bailey, my sidekick and assistant, who lasted the saddle sores and long miles till the end of the trail. Also to Dave Harrel for help and support thoughout the shoot.

MICHAEL RUTHERFORD

Text Sources

Many of the cowboys who appear in this book shared their thoughts and feelings with the photographer in tape-recorded conversations. Those conversations were the source for the quotes that appear on the following pages: 42, 49, 53, 74, 82, 109, 127, 134, 172. Other sources are: 32: Twain, Mark, *Roughing It.* Harper & Brothers, 1913; 37, 152: Halsell, HH., *Cowboys and Cattleland.* Texas Christian University Press, 1983; 44: Leakey, John, as told to Nellie Snyder Yost, *The West That Was.* Southern Methodist University Press, 1958. University of Nebraska Press, 1976; 70: Lanning, Jim and Judy, Eds., *Texas Cowboys: Memories of the Early Days.* Texas A&M University Press, 1984; 84: Linderman, Frank Bird, *Recollections of Charley Russell.* University of Oklahoma Press, 1963; 90, 164: Kiskadoon, Bruce, *Rhymes of the Ranges,* 1947. Gibbs Smith Publishing, 1987; 95: Harte, Bret, *A Waif of the Plains.* Houghton-Mifflin, 1896; 114: Rollins, Philip Aston, *The Cowboy.* Scribner's, 1922; 129: Roosevelt, Theodore, *The Cattle Country of the Far West.* Scribner's, 1926; 146: Remington, Fredric. "In the Sierra Nevada with the Punchers." *Harper's Monthly,* Feb., 1894; 167: Roosevelt, Theodore, *Ranch Life and the Hunting Trail.* Century, 1888; 174: Wister, Owen, *The Virginian.* Macmillan, 1904.

Photo Credits

All of the color photographs are courtesy of Rutherford Studios, Nashville, Tennessee. The black and white photos were graciously supplied by the following: American Heritage Center, University of Wyoming 23, 60, 61, 64; Amon Carter Museum, Fort Worth 100, 140; Barker Texas History Center, University of Texas at Austin 58; Boot Hill Museum Inc., Dodge City, Ks. 21 (right); Thomas B. Curtis and Susan Ross Curtis, from the collection of Nellie Miller Glasgow 62; The Kobal Collection 18; Library of Congress 20, 99, 138; Montana Historical Society 63; Erwin Smith Collection of the Library of Congress on deposit at the Amon Carter Museum 143; South Dakota Historical Society 21 (left); Wyoming State Archives, Museums, and Historical Department 19, 22, 59, 98, 101, 103, 139, 141.

An M&M Book

Project Director & Editor   Gary Fishgall

Photo Research   Ben McLaughlin, Lucinda Stellini; *Literary Research*   Ben McLaughlin

Senior Editorial Assistant   Shirley Vierheller; *Editorial Assistant*   Lisa Pike;

Copy Editor   Bert N. Zelman of Publishers Workshop Inc.

Designer   Binns & Lubin/Betty Binns

Separations and Printing   Regent Publishing Services Ltd.

Typesetting   Sharon Brant Typography

To cowboys . . . and all that that implies.

JAMES BRIDGES
Urban Cowboy (movie)